the effects of dry chamomile

elyssia koulouris

Illustrated by Sam Paverd

First published by Busybird Publishing 2021

Copyright © 2021 Elyssia Koulouris

ISBN
978-1-922465-61-0 (paperback)
978-1-922465-62-7 (ebook)

This work is copyright. Apart from any use permitted under the *Copyright Act 1968*, no part of this publication may be reproduced, stored in a retrieval system or transmitted in any form or by any means, electronic, mechanical, photocopying, recording or otherwise, without the prior written permission of Elyssia Koulouris.

Cover Image: Sam Paverd
Cover design: Busybird Publishing
Layout and typesetting: Busybird Publishing
Illustrations: Sam Paverd

Busybird Publishing
2/118 Para Road
Montmorency, Victoria
Australia 3094

www.busybird.com.au

*Dedicated to
my Grandparents (pappous kai giagia)
and those who took the risk of a lifetime
and bravely became the essence of the
Australian Dream.*

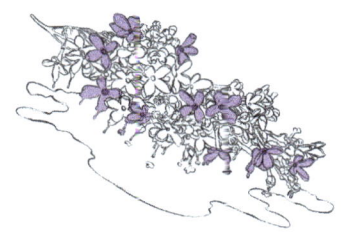

Breakfast

You changed the height restriction without telling me
A disappointed child too short to ride
I needed to grow first
For you
My favourite ice-cream flavour ran low
I settled for chocolate, dark and bitter
I knew how to adapt
For you I could

The ability to hold my neck up alone, wilted
Slowly like the perfume of a lilac
If you spared

            a drop

                        of water

You couldn't give as you rested from taking

Even though you just made me

scrambled eggs

Maple Syrup

Soaking you in my love
French toast floating in eggs
Smells sweet
As you flip me over
Printing my neck with your lips

Purple Haze

temptation of honey
drizzles onto fried cheese
oozes from his open mouth
                      like gold lust

moon bulb eyes project purple haze
like hot blueberries swimming in pancake batter
drips slowly but surely
                leaves a thick film over my body like an oily
blanket over the ocean

richer with age are whiskey words that swallow me
into an early grave of regret
but I happily drink
                like a woman deprived of flakes of flattery

hand as smooth as melted butter dissolves into the warmth of a pan
seeps into my thigh skin as his voice drowns the echoes of others
my index finger rests on my bottom lip as he shares
                stories that taste like our future endeavours

intrigue pricks my lower back like thorns piercing silk
dangers hook
wraps around my neck
                like daisy chains

He
        Tastes
                Like
                        Honey

Artichokes

Peel my outer set of leaves
Expose my stem
Make me safe to taste
Use something pointed
To slice
Smear me delicately in butter
Salt to make me thirsty
Simmer me gently
And you will see
The softness of my inner leaf

Icarus

Don't fly too close to the sun

the honey you spread on your toast

this morning

will burn if you leave it

like the boils on your scalp

that you pick

till they bleed

syrup on my pancakes

but you dissolve

like sugar in my coffee

a foolish lamb

I told you

it would stick

like molasses

Don't fly too close to the sun

your raw underneath

skin flutters as you fall

like salty corn flakes

Cravings

I eat jam out of the jar. Only pink jam. The strawberry or the raspberry. I don't like toast. I tell myself a teaspoon is nothing. A teaspoon is irrelevant. A teaspoon is a tea spoon. The sugar lathers my taste buds I like the chunks of pro cessed fruit frozen within the jelly Sweet or savoury. Al ways. Un til. My tongue throbs for a taste of diff er ence.

Nothing can replace

      the taste

           of him

Self esteem

Like butter smeared onto toast
molten gold
Dissolves
Into taste

Lust

pomegranate
bleeds from lips
stained cheeks
exposure forced
inside of a fig
freckles the
beauty spot above your lip
rub my back to sleep
the touch of a blackberry's skin
cushions me in cotton
more like a father than a lover

Olives

Thumb nails that dig into my skin
Unwrap my outer layer
It gently falls to the floor like silk sheets
That flap on clothes lines in summer

Exposed to lust filled air
Smells like fields of chamomile
Lingers
As tips of fingers

Outline the imperfections of the pip

Milk Caps

She told me that her grandmother used to hoard the gold and
red caps

The bottled branded M
Wash and return
600ml
She said it didn't mean anything

Her silver hair blinded her left eye, her head
Did that judgmental tilt when I said
"I am using it as a flower pot"

The verbena sprouted as though its seed knew to follow the
glass formation
The bottom was still scarred with rust, I tried to pick it off with my
finger-nails like the skin
Left over from a

Popped pimple
No success
It sits on the birds-eye maple
stained by a ring that I can't scrub off

Wild fire

you spread through me like chamomile fields lit on fire

                                        I refuse to burn since you left me

gems in my cupboard
your gaze
control
hands
this is why you asked me here
I would've been satisfied with

                                        you sitting on the corner of my bed

telling me what you had for dinner
your words
my ears
kindling light
your breath had a hint of garlic

prayer positioned hands

                                        between my knees open my legs

one

quick

motion

my mind lags

my body shapes

with you

                                        spread through me like runny eggs on toast

The Effects of Dry Chamomile

My tongue burns

                I sip chamomile tea

Too quickly

                To soothe my thoughts

I've said it before

                Coated in your past

In left over chamomile fields

                That crinkle between my toes

Chamomile seeds

                Delicately the size of

That beauty spot above my lip

                You stare in adoration

As though it were a mark

                From your finger tip

The harsh winters hit our bones

                Rattle our cages

Until we forget

        The smell of summer

You tell me to keep

        The chamomile flowers

In a cotton cloth to place under

        My pillow for sweet summer dreams

You don't seem to mind the mess

        You never seem to mind

A warm smirk of pride

        Creases your mouth

The way cinnamon warmth

        Rises from your Bolognese

We dance in the kitchen

        In chamomile dreams

Stepping off the boat

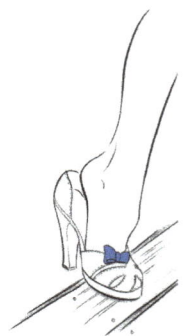

when she stepped off the boat her heel got caught between cracks in the decking Moon Bulb eyes of a stranger under an officer hat NAVY AUTHORITY liquid lust oozes out of his mouth she gathers herself shoulders back CONFIDENT she tip toes toward him his stare pollutes her stride leaving a thick film of oil over the ocean she mustn't snap or sneer at him NO NO NO NO she must NOT she must NOT let him murk her new home water she wondered if wearing a linen dress showing her calves was risqué she wondered if wearing makeup after a 6 week journey was a mistake she thought then the low tone of his voice drips down the back of her neck like sap trickling down bark in summer his voice drowns the echoes of others she turns to face him his index finger touches her bottom lip her lips purse the same way they do after a shot of whiskey but still she stares thinking of the home she left the home to create the home within she didn't say a word but became the full essence of femme strength which perfumed onto him to such a degree he let go of her lip she stepped back to observe his reaction out of curiosity not fear then walked past him in triumph following a crowd of foreign strangers like her who lead her to a bus stop she waited so tired very hungry and scared she opened her suitcase and picked up an envelope opened it her fingers traced along the address she exhaled and really hope someone made some decent coffee

Grandmother Rose

Her fingers curve around the handle of the cup as she places English breakfast tea on discoloured doilies. Her gold tea set, something I wish to inherit, mocks me on the table. Her right hand rests near the doily, taking a much needed break from the lifting of the tea cup – the strenuousness of it.

The simple act that was once not even a fleeting thought is now a visible discomfort in rough fingers that once kneaded buttery dough, cupped my face and pegged table cloths. I look at the lines on her face while I sip the comforting familiarity of too much sugar and milk in tea. It warms like her famous chicken and rice, upon my entrance.

She bends from her waist to sit, reminding me of my ballet class. Working on the barre, slow, steady, tense yet graceful as I plie down shielding my inner strain. She attempts to hide the discomfort in her hip, but fails the way I do in hiding my emotions. She could always read my face like a detailed page, now I can read hers.

My eyes linger on her face and I fear the inevitability of my future. Discomfort stings in my stomach and I adjust my posture. Her face is worn like my leather wallet but the distraction of her eyes, as green as the fields she ran her fingers through as a little village girl, comfort me.

In her eyes I see the glistening green eyes of trauma of a child who was taken from her mother, and sent to Serbia. Though she learned classical piano and can still remember those four, learned languages, when she returned to her mother years later, she was dismissed like an unwanted pest.

As we hold each other's gaze – her eyes green, mine brown – I think of her desperation as clear as the wrinkles on her face. That desperation turned to wanting, turned to seeking a dream, turned to actively taking that first step on to the ship that brought her to Australia.

Yiayia went to church

Yiayia went to church dressed in a silk green suit
Yiayia went to church with bright red nail polish
Yiayia went to church looking like a Christmas tree
Yiayia went to church with outside eyes scanning her
Yiayia went to church to see answers in priest's eyes
Yiayia went to church when her cancer spread
Yiayia went to church and forgot how she got there
Yiayia went to church and stood alone
Yiayia went to church to pray
Yiayia went to church to speak to Papou
Yiayia went to church to beg for a cure
Yiayia went to church to feel purpose
Yiayia went to church to sip wine
Yiayia went to church to hide
Yiayia went to church with bruised sockets
Yiayia went to church with a broken arm
Yiayia went to church with a baby
Yiayia went to church to cradle a bible
Yiayia went to church to sing
Yiayia went to church for a christening
Yiayia went to church for a wedding
Yiayia went to church for a funeral
Yiayia went to church to find home
Yiayia was carried to church so I could say goodbye

Beginnings

a mother endures morning sickness
before the baby comes
a dancer wraps her toes
with tape
a seamstress licks the thread
before insertion
a gardener plants the seed
for it to grow
an artist mixes colours
before putting brush to canvas
my Grandfather's patience
pricks him before he picks the cherries

The bird

What happens when a bird is silenced?
Do the other birds sing their songs?
Ten times as loud
To make up for its loss?

What happens when a bird is plucked bald?
Do the others shower it in feathers found?
Ten times as warm
To make up for its nakedness?

She looked from head to toe
Like she was something to loathe
And I stood silent
To make up for what?

She stood fluttering her feathers
Full of femininity
Pliers at the ready

Nest

you swoop
you nestle me back
into the imprint I once made
drop me into your comfort
twigs pierce my skin
mud fogs my rationale
leaves are itching
my heart races
like it did
when
you
cared
or
didn't
toes curl as your finger outlines my lips
euphoria stings
prick

Goodbye

tell you something

don't   hear me out

            open your mouth

make me think

                                            twice

                    your grip

something   I've resented

            like going to the dentist

my teeth   sawdust   thin

I called you   favourite

            in the world

disconnected

no respect	no response
can't look at me	I look at you
	with regret
my first	it's hard for me to say
unveil your goodness	talking slow
regret	final
	let me go

New relationships

deprived
of
understanding
I
starve
you
feast
without
sparing
a
drop
I
wilt
without
sun
sun
offered
on
a
silver
platter
by
a
new
moon
you
orbit
out
of
sight

Past Puddles

sky cries I follow leaving puddles
of our past on the foot path
I sprint
maybe it was dramatic
the memory of us
look to the future
tongue stings
champagne bubbles
fuck
I replay

My body an open book
his carelessness crinkles the pages.
He longs for the momentary high

Turn

She asks him where he grew up
He doesn't say
She asks him about his family
Confession starts
She asks him how he feels
Her empathy creeps in earlier than expected
She asks him if he thinks she's different now
He said he is damaged goods

She is a collector

Pains

dissolved into his sponge
then drained
all talk no action
or
all action no talk
gluttony replaces his eye sockets
dependant on everlasting warmth
leaving victims cold

Aches

for your cocoon
familiar cloud
nestled in the same place necks intertwined
as you flick through the channels
my eyes flutter and
close
the footy is on

Purity

The sky cries messily
Like the pool I leave in the sink
Tap running
Tears running
Weighing my chest down
Brick by brick

My eyes asked questions
No answer
Seeped from me like sap
Uncontrollable
Stung with a reality check

Bathing in my milk-like mind
You rinsed my hair clean
The water below left pure

Residue

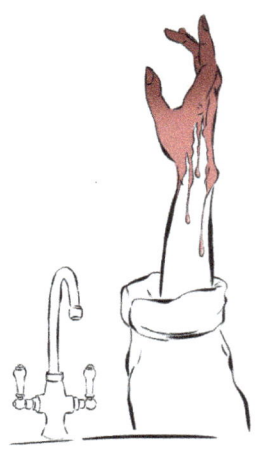

Peel cherry skin
Lay me with fingers stained

Coat me in Morning Fresh
Leave me to drip dry

Dimple my butter lips
Spread me onto toast *melted*

Dress me with milk
A wanted purity

Strain to see
Me pouring down the sink

Like a left over bottle of champagne from the night before

Rounds

packaged candy
Drink
unwrapped and inhaled
Drink
been *inserted here*
Drink

Forms of flattery

Mirror me
Thine enemy
Mirror me
Well
Mirror me
With evil

Know it well
Mirror me

As you

mirror me
and melt gold to lather
mirror me
prick my finger and paint thy lips
mirror me
dipping in innocence
flattery flatter flat
stretch the lace
salt water drips through
stings face
mirror me

The one-dimensional girl

Like branded cattle
Like that dirty plate
you leave in the dishwasher
to wash over
and over again
Until that chunk of food
disappears
Until it's colourless
Pale as marble
Stripped of character
Like the red wine
imprinted on your lace table cloth
Bleached
You hold me under
your vinegar grip
And force me to
taste your insecurity until
I fall victim to your bitterness
I
the girl
tired of the scab that you pick at
to delay its healing
and induce to scar
delaying the inevitable

Envy

a white rose
40 petals
you pick them
my skin sheds
the stem

You make men feel special just by talking to them
an attempt to seduce me
one button at a time

you have been
on this earth
longer than I
yet you pray
for me to tumble
like a child
parading in her mother's heels

with a heavy heart
I apologise
wide eyes,
sick stomach
It isn't my fault! I am sorry but you are the wonderful one
you turn your back to me

I lie in my oasis
draped in roses
thorns graze my skin
a stamp

a shout
I am pierced
my perfume drips
blood

with your finger you
steal a drop
place it on your tongue
satisfied
So sweet you grin

you have been on this earth
long enough to know better

Rouge

it is not he
whose lust glistens like diamonds in his eyes

nor her
oozing rouge of sexuality

he strips
her down to olive skin

he catches
the warmth seeping from her mouth

he glides
through time with a child's essence down her spine

she cares
little for his shell

the man
between his ears she holds with golden hands

it is not he
who glues petals onto a rose

but he who can withstand the winter

Scarlet

naivety my crown of thorns
picked my scalp
the wise woman, bleeding
forced to stomach your corset of lust
the wise woman, captured

Beer

I could drink a glass of you
        right now
and glaze my mind
of wondering eyes
something small but strong
        to blur my sight
shiver down my spine
exhale to let go of the words
numbed by fears unsaid
        or maybe something tall and cold
        like the Heineken in your hand
words will slur
        through half closed eyes
a cigarette behind your ear
        in which I whisper
what I am wearing underneath
sip through the foamy cloud above
drink the oaky liquid quick
Then maybe you'll tell me its all real

The Egoist's Child

An oar floating in a river
Plucked like a green tomato
On the brink of readiness

The soil was fertile as the rain
Made it puddle
The drops echoed into your narcissism
Giving *me* what you needed

I ran into the river
While you stared at your reflection
An oar in the river
We are lost
I float with my olive sized companion

For sale

A house
In need of
Renovation
Cracked unstable
Damaged from before
And again

>Question: was the door ever open?
>Question: was it a tease like a fly-screen?
>To peep inside but never break through
>Too many questions

I offered you everything
I had on my sleeve
Wide-eyed the same way
I'd offer my sleeve as a child to
Impatient children
Waiting for someone better
To play with
Settled for a while without me
And it was pleasant
For a while
Came back
I knew
And I was reminded of
Feeling as

>empty as a house

A special thank you to my family and friends for their endless love and support through this creative journey.

A special thank you to Dr Nadia Niaz for helping me with my thesis at The University of Melbourne and whose extensive knowledge, gusto and patience influenced by work immensely.

About the Author

Elyssia Koulouris is an actor/writer based in Melbourne, Australia and Los Angeles. She has an Arts degree along with a Masters in Creative Writing, Publishing and Editing from the University of Melbourne. Elyssia's work explores the feminine identity in relationships, healing, the migrant experience, and the Greek culture. This is her first collection of poetry.

www.ingramcontent.com/pod-product-compliance
Lightning Source LLC
Chambersburg PA
CBHW040418100526
44588CB00022B/2865